SAINT LOUIS UNIVERSITY

A CONCISE HISTORY (1818–2008)

Saint Louis University

A Concise History (1818–2008)

William Barnaby Faherty, S.J.

Gas House Books

PO Box 5131,

St. Louis, MO 63139, USA

Contemporary photographs by Mark Scott Abeln

Library of Congress Control Number: on file

ISBN: 978-0-9800475-4-7

Please visit our website at www.reedypress.com.

Printed in the United States of America

09 10 11 12 13   5 4 3 2 1

CONTENTS

Foreword

by Daniel C. O'Connell, S.J.

vii

Saint Louis University:

A Concise History

1

FOREWORD

DANIEL C. O'CONNELL, S.J.

28TH PRESIDENT OF THE UNIVERSITY

It's now been a considerable time since a diocesan priest opened classes at the Saint Louis Academy, located in what is now downtown St. Louis—191 years, to be exact. And for fully one half of all those years, Father William B. Faherty, S.J., has been sojourning on this earth. For an astounding seventy-eight of his years,

WILLIAM BARNABY FAHERTY, S.J.

he has been associated with this venerable institution, known today as Saint Louis University. Even during the years when he was deeply engaged at other locations, including a number of other Jesuit institutions and the Kennedy Space Center, Saint Louis University always remained for him a special place with special people—his academic home base.

And now, as if in preparation for the University's bicentenary, Father Faherty has summed up for us the history of Saint Louis University, filled with accomplishments and travails. No one can claim a better background for the task than this nonagenarian Jesuit priest. St. Louis, Missouri, has been his lifetime historical preoccupation: Everything that has had anything to do with this city and her people—from soccer to saintliness, from being Irish to being German, from the Missouri Botanical Garden to Visitation Academy—has become subject

WILLIAM BARNABY FAHERTY, S.J.

matter for his historical pen. From a number of very different assignments—not to speak of his initiation into Jesuit learning as a student at Saint Louis University High School (Class of '31)—editorial responsibilities at the Queen's Work publishing apostolate, curator's tasks at the Museum of Western Jesuit Missions, archivist at the Midwest Jesuit Archives, radio commentator on things "St. Louis" and—many years ago—the roles of student, alumnus, and finally, professor at Saint Louis University, he has accumulated the story of his beloved University. He comes, too, with the authorship of well over thirty books under his belt and a set of wonderfully benevolent biases: He loved Saint Louis University's Parks College; he admires especially Father William B. Rogers, S.J., the "second founder" of Saint Louis University, as well as the pioneer leaders of the University. He knows why some pro-

WILLIAM BARNABY FAHERTY, S.J.

grams have worked and why some have been dismal failures—he was there.

For many years now—both during and after my years as student, professor, and administrator at Saint Louis University—I have become increasingly appreciative of and grateful for Father Faherty's spiritual, academic, and personal inspiration in my own life.

Read Father Faherty's fond portrayal of the first chartered university west of the Mississippi. Learn to know and love Saint Louis University. And if you are blessed enough to call her your alma mater, be grateful and justifiably proud of what she has meant to all of us—to the City of St. Louis, the nation, and the world at large! Relish her twenty-first-century mid-city presence and her hopes for continuing this dedicated service far into the future. Thanks

WILLIAM BARNABY FAHERTY, S.J.

to Father Faherty's scholarly pen, all she has been is here.

Father Daniel C. O'Connell, S.J.

WILLIAM BARNABY FAHERTY, S.J.

SAINT LOUIS UNIVERSITY

A CONCISE HISTORY (1818–2008)

SAINT LOUIS
UNIVERSITY:
A CONCISE
HISTORY

Saint Louis University claims its origin in 1818, when Bishop William V. DuBourg started a small college in St. Louis. The Jesuits took over in 1827 and began classes in 1829. Walter Hill, historian, wrote a history of Saint Louis University on its fiftieth anniversary. That was in 1879, fifty years after the Jesuits started teaching in 1829. William Fanning, a historian of the next generation, went back to the original 1818. The one con-

WILLIAM BARNABY FAHERTY, S.J.

tinuity between the first group and the second was the student body. Even today, people have disagreements on this issue. Be that as it may, Bishop DuBourg started a small school in 1818 under the direction of Francois Niel, the first priest ordained in St. Louis.

In early years, a qualified, experienced lay teacher, Elihu Shepard, taught many young men at the school who distinguished themselves in the early West. Then Father Niel returned to France and Father Edmund Saulnier, the pastor, kept the school alive as best he could. In 1827, the new bishop of St. Louis, Joseph Rosati, asked the Jesuits, who had begun a combined Indian school and seminary at Florissant, to staff the school. This they did, under Father Charles Felix van Quickenborne, who promoted the school among businessmen, Catholic and Protestant. A large four-story building went up at Ninth and Christy, on the

William V. DuBourg

WILLIAM BARNABY FAHERTY, S.J.

5

second terrace back from the Mississippi, a commanding site at the time.

A few years later, the Jesuit General sent a special visitor with plenipotentiary power, Peter Kenney, a distinguished member of the Irish province who had testified before Parliament in the interests of the Irish Jesuits and had an impressive career otherwise.

He faced several basic issues. With so few Jesuits, was it of value to keep them busy with the education of a few young men, in contrast with the great work that they do as circuit-riding missionaries establishing parishes among the immigrants who had swarmed into the area, especially at that time, northern Illinois? Kenney gave much thought to this issue. He finally decided that it was worthwhile to keep the school but that the other work could be done by several specialists.

Kenney had heard of the severity of the Missouri mission superiors. He put in place a young man, Peter Verhaegen. He was the youngest president of Saint Louis University in its history and was to prove one of the most able. At the advice of Senator Thomas Hart Benton, he asked for a state charter that allowed a future expansion in medicine and law. This, Governor Daniel Dunklin granted in 1832. Thus, Saint Louis University became the first university chartered west of the Mississippi.

Father John Elet succeeded Verhaegen. Like his predecessor, John Elet was a man of pleasant personality and balanced judgment. Physically, he was exactly the opposite. The small, prim, and handsome-featured Elet contrasted sharply with the large, vigorous, and now-portly Verhaegen.

With the presidential appointment of James Oliver van der Velde in 1840, Saint

Louis University could justly claim the best-educated college president in the United States. Most contemporary college administrators had a slight acquaintance with the classics and limited training in theology at the school they later headed. Van der Velde had studied and taught in Belgium and at the Georgetown College before teaching at Saint Louis University.

He read and spoke Latin and was fluent in Flemish, English, French, Italian, and Spanish. He gave public addresses in all these languages. His few published lectures show correct use of words, strict grammatical structure, and good taste in all elements that combine to make a finished composition. He brought Saint Louis University to a position of eminence it never again matched in that century, and perhaps in all its history.

WILLIAM BARNABY FAHERTY, S.J.

The medical school got underway during his term, and he also brought in Judge Richard Buckner from Kentucky, who began lectures in law.

In 1840, when Saint Louis University had the best-educated university president in the country, it could also boast of having the best classical scholar, Peter Arnoudt, who put together a Greek grammar and a collection of Greek short poetry and an epic poem of 1,200 verses in Greek. He also composed a 735-page spiritual guidebook in Latin called *The Imitation of the Sacred Heart*, patterned after the time-tested *Imitation of Christ* by Thomas á Kempis, a Belgian of an earlier century. Arnoudt's book actually had characteristics that earlier work lacked, especially a positive view of apostolic work. Nonetheless, a general of the Jesuits, John Roothaan, held this book up, and only after he passed on did his successor, a

Belgian like Arnoudt, approve the book. It went into nine languages and is still available in English in paperback today.

Father George L. Carrell was the first American-born Jesuit to be president of Saint Louis University. After he finished his term of four years, he was named bishop of Covington in Kentucky.

The next president, John Baptist Druyts, contrasted sharply with the far-reaching and wide-roving fellow Jesuits of those early days. While Father Peter de Smet was getting ready to go among the Native Americans, Druyts never left St. Louis. From the time he came, finished his studies, and taught, he was always at Saint Louis University. He taught, became dean, and then president. Steady progress was made in every area.

Unfortunately, at that time a burst of

Nativism turned against all immigrants. These Nativists threatened Saint Louis University, and especially the two buildings of classical style that benefactor John O'Fallon had built for his son-in-law, Dr. Charles Alexander Pope, dean of the medical school. When some of the doctors, fearful of the Nativists, wanted to withdraw the school from the University, Druyts said, "If you withdraw, I will get other doctors." He defied the Nativists.

His successor, John Verdin, a native of St. Louis of French-Irish background, and a more conciliatory man, gave in to the request of the medical faculty. They went independent. John O'Fallon, who had aided the University with the two medical buildings, soon gave his attention to a newly founded Washington University. He promoted a technical school that became the basis later of Washington University's School of Engineering. It was to the detriment of both groups that the disaffiliation occurred.

Before the Civil War, besides local students many resident students came from Louisiana. As a result, when the Civil War began, many students withdrew. Most of the officers among the alums of Saint Louis University were Southerners, including John George Walker, who came to the aid of Stonewall Jackson at Antietam.

After this battle, he became a major general and was sent to a more quiet section in the West. For the rest of the war, he served in obscurity. At its end, he lived outstate.

During the course of the war, Father Ferdinand Cuosemans headed the University. He was succeeded in the presidency in 1862 by Thomas O'Neal. Born in Ireland, O'Neal had come to St. Louis at the invitation of his uncle, John Edward Walsh, presumably to pursue a business career with him. O'Neal entered the school in the commercial course, but before he completed his course, he became convinced that his vocation lay in the priesthood. He studied philosophy in Rome and theology at Fordham and taught for a while at a school for Jesuits in North St. Louis that came to be called College Hill. Then, in 1862, he became president of Saint Louis University.

While a two-year-old city university in St. Louis at Sixteenth and Pine did not re-open in the fall of 1861, and the total faculty of Missouri Medical College left for the South, Saint Louis University continued. The school enrolled increased numbers in 1862. Father O'Neal obtained draft exemptions for the students. Further, Father O'Neal felt the nine-foot wall around the school made it looked too much like a correctional institution. And there was much talk of getting a campus elsewhere.

The last half of the nineteenth century saw little advance for Saint Louis University. Even the move in 1889 to a Grand Avenue site at the west end of the city did not dispel the strict regime of the school. In the meanwhile, the Christian Brothers College began in 1855 and taught Latin with the permission of the Pope. The school flourished and moved west on Easton at Kingshighway. The Brothers built a substantial and impressive building.

The one effort of importance in that last fifty years of Saint Louis University downtown was the graduate lecture program sponsored by Thomas Hughes, an English-born Jesuit historian. He arranged for this program of graduate lectures that brought considerable attention and excellent attendance. When a new provincial, Father John

Frieden, headed the Province, however, he removed Father Hughes from the University and sent him on different high school assignments for successive years. In 1894, a new provincial, Father Thomas Fitzgerald, asked Hughes if he were willing to join a Jesuit historians group in Italy. The following year Hughes left for Rome, where he wrote *The history of the Society of Jesus in North America, Colonial and Federal.* This work brought the most distinguished award ever won by a Jesuit, the second Loubat prize given by Columbia University.

The late years of the century were grim days under Father Joseph Grimmelsman. His biggest mistake was to reject the offer of a group of Catholic doctors to become part of Saint Louis University. They staffed the Missouri Medical College and worked with Mercy Sisters at their hospital. He could not see his way. The doctors joined up with Saint Louis University's original medical school, now the Saint Louis College of Medicine, to form Washington University's Medical College.

At the turn of the century, the most significant man in the history of Saint Louis University, William Banks Rogers, a native of Kentucky, brought the old college into alignment with the realities of American academic development and enlarged its scope and vision. Though unprepossessing in appearance, he had the qualities of a major educator. He displayed a concern for public image that many of his confreres lacked. He fought the over-concentration on the classical tradition and the growing power and independent purposes of the "scholasticate establishment," the professors who taught the Jesuit seminarians. Rogers fought them all and won. He rightly could be called the second founder of Saint Louis University

WILLIAM BARNABY FAHERTY, S.J.

At the same time, the youthful archbishop of St. Louis, John J. Glennon, was giving to the archdiocese the vigor Rogers gave to the University.

Rogers won the support of the local clergy by extending tuition privileges to various parish schools. He updated the Americanization of terms used on campus. He gave Saint Louis University High School its own corporate existence and separated the faculties.

Rogers wanted to affiliate a medical school and had to go look for one. He found two young schools that had just united, and he brought them into the orbit of the University. One could only ask, why had Grimmelsman hesitated? Rogers went out and secured the money to buy these two medical schools.

Rogers brought in a highly promising football coach from Wisconsin, Eddie Cochems, who built Midwestern champions. His team played against the legendary Jim Thorpe of the Carlisle Indians.

The University placed a full-page advertisement in the World's Fair Guide and had a booth in the Palace of Education. But even before that, it had invited President Theodore Roosevelt to give a talk when he came to dedicate the Exposition in the fall of 1903. He spoke at the University. James Cardinal Gibbons also attended that event. Rogers welcomed educators from all over the country who at this meeting formed the American Catholic Education Association.

Father Thomas Ewing Sherman, the orator and son of the general, gave a stirring talk at one of the meetings of the Catholic Educational Association on the need of Catholic women, especially teachers, religious and lay, to attend the universities. Unfortunately, Sherman's words went unheeded for many years. Even Rogers did not invite coeds to the campus.

In the education of Jesuits, Rogers felt that the professors spent all their time on Catholic viewpoints and failed to give the students a look at the wider attitudes and beliefs of other philosophers and educators. In fact, he ran headlong into the scholasticate establishment. He more than held his own. He gathered a number of prominent businessmen as consultants: John Scullin, Festus Wade, Paul Bakewell, Julius Walsh, and others.

Some of the energy of the Rogers period continued during the time of Father John Frieden. Nine of the twelve members of the original Advisory Board agreed to serve again. Frieden commissioned Father James Conway to open a law school.

Father Joseph Davis, professor of English, came to the fore at this time. He commented on the weather with the formality of a papal decree. Such mannerisms made him a "character" on campus. His amazing business sense made him a unique character among clergymen.

He planned a school of Commerce and Finance similar to that at Columbia University, to offer advanced courses in business. To get the school underway, he solicited pledges from a number of local businessmen to meet the initial expenses. No doubt these men were pleasantly surprised that they did not have to redeem their pledges. The school moved on a solid financial road from its outset. George W. Wilson, vice president of Mercantile Trust Company, became the

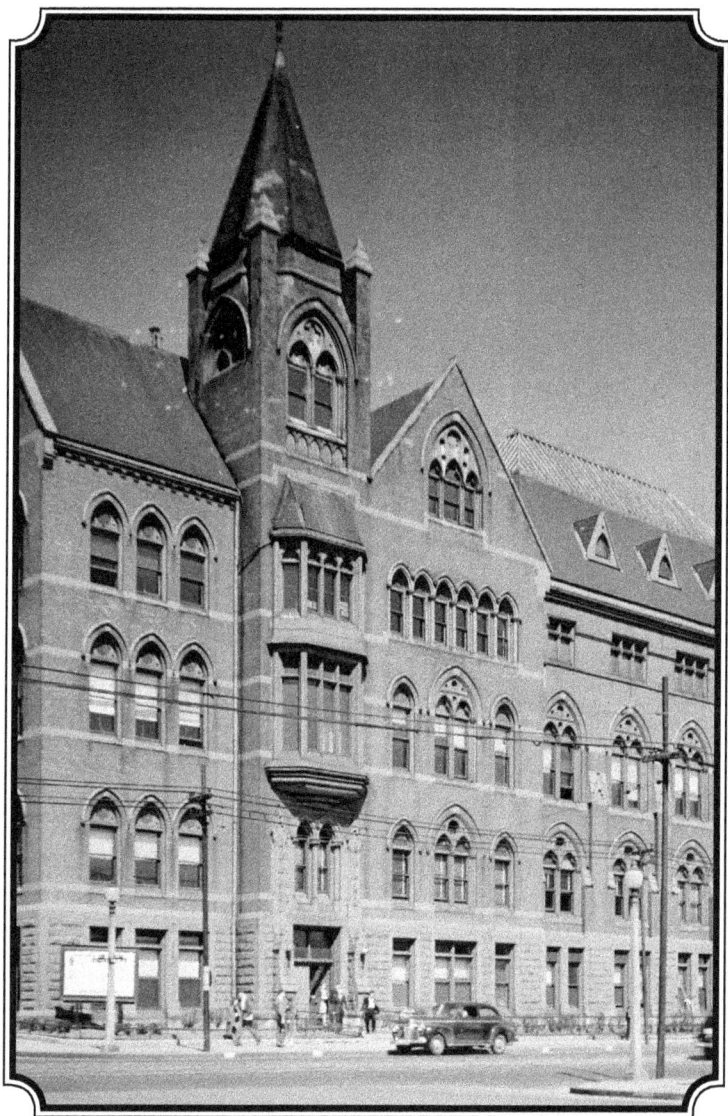

DuBourg Hall

WILLIAM BARNABY FAHERTY, S.J.

21

first dean. The teachers came from the business community and also from other schools of the University such as law, theology, and philosophy, among them Father O'Boyle, who had been chancellor under Father Rogers. While the professional schools of Medicine, Law, and Dentistry moved to a graduate status, Commerce and Finance offered an alternative to Liberal Arts on the undergraduate level. Many fellow faculty members took a dim view of this inaugural.

In spite of difficulties "internal, external and fraternal," as Father Davis described them, he and his associates developed an excellent school in the University. During the last years of World War, Father Davis directed a program of Student Army Training corps under the command of Captain Henry Gimmel. The soldiers drilled in the college quadrangle, and Father Davis directed this program. Likewise, when the war was over, Father Davis arranged for retraining ex-servicemen. The Veterans Bureau eventually sent four hundred men for accounting and other courses over a two-year period.

On September 23, 1926, St. Louis businessman Martin Shaughnessy died. He left in trust holdings valued at about $1.5 million. One-half of this was to become available to the Commerce and Finance School at Saint Louis University after the death of his wife. The University earmarked part of this gift for a new school of Commerce and Finance, the Davis-Shaughnessy Hall on Lindell. In the will, interestingly, Shaughnessy had stressed competence in the vernacular as an instrument in business success.

In the 1920s, the "Corporate College" arrangement whereby Webster, Maryville, and Fontbonne, the three Catholic colleges in the area, and the community colleges formed by different sisterhoods, became part of the University. The students of Maryville and these other schools took part in intramural activities and received their degrees from Saint Louis University. It was a blessing for all of them and continued for a period of twenty years.

This expanse of time was called by some observers as the period of the independent Duchies, with Father Alphonse Schwitalla in Medicine, Linus Lilly in Law, Thomas Knapp in Arts, and the already-mentioned Joseph Davis in Business.

Father Bernard Dempsey, whose doctorate from Harvard was in Economics, and Murray Cantwell eventually replaced the original team of Regent Davis and Dean Wilson. Father Davis died in 1939.

Class of 1936 on its fiftieth reunion

WILLIAM BARNABY FAHERTY, S.J.

The University presidents in those years, nice men that they were, were generally not public figures: Father Charles Cloud, an unusually handsome man, and then Robert Johnson, of a prominent family in Milwaukee.

Two Jesuit activities that began at the University, but eventually moved their offices a block or two away, also gained prestige at the time. The National Sodality Service Center, under the direction of Daniel A. Lord, promoted a popular religious organization, the Sodality of Our Lady. The Center published widely read religious literature. Lord had been the faculty sponsor of the University paper when it took the name *University News* back in 1920, with Claude Heithaus, a member of the senior class, the editor. The sodalities were active on campus, with Father Benjamin Fulkerson directing the women, Father Ed Finn guiding men in the Arts College, and Father Joseph Boland leading those in the Commerce School.

The locally influential Laymen's Retreat League, headed by James P. Monaghan, opened a center of recollection on the bluffs above the Mississippi River south of the city. He, too, had offices on the University campus for a time.

In June 1943, Patrick J. Holloran, son of a St. Louis businessman, became the twenty-sixth president of Saint Louis University. He had taught in the seminary section of the University, the Jesuit School of Philosophy. The teachers of Theology had moved to St. Mary's, Kansas, in 1931, but they remained a branch of the University. To many, in fact, the secular section of the school seemed an appendage of the seminary. The vast majority of distinguished alumni had been Jesuits, especially professors and presidents of all Jesuit universities in the Midwest and the South. University presidents at the time also directed the large Jesuit communities.

Holloran's first public gesture was an expression of welcome to coeds, the first enthusiastic greeting the women on the campus had ever enjoyed. Many Jesuit presidents still thought that women should have stayed at the local Catholic women's colleges. A second gesture was to confer an honorary Doctor of Law on the Dean Emeritus of the School of Commerce, George W. Wilson, former president of Mercantile Trust Company.

It was at this time that Father Holloran wrote to a group of Catholic businessmen, Oliver Parks, the founder of Parks College of Aeronautical Engineers at Cahokia, Illinois, among them, to ask their opinion on the question of integrating the faculty and student body. The provincial superior of the Jesuits of the region, the Very Reverend Peter A. Brooks, S.J., had offered this difficult challenge to Father Holloran. Father Brooks recommended that the University explore the possibility of opening to them at that time. Father Claude Heithaus, professor of anthropology, had returned from the Middle East with a great knowledge of the early sites and forgotten places. He was public relations director of the University and faculty sponsor for the school paper, the *University News*. He had originally edited it under the direction of faculty sponsor Daniel A. Lord, back in 1920.

The *University News* for February 13, 1944, under the editorship of Jack Maguire, later a prominent priest of the St. Louis Archdiocese, carried the sermon that Heithaus gave at the mandatory students' mass at 11:00 on that day. Few men besides

Father Claude Heithaus

WILLIAM BARNABY FAHERTY, S.J.

Jack Maguire and two or three other pre-draft freshmen were in attendance. Most in the full church were women students.

Father Heithaus challenged them to treat the blacks well, and in a calm, deliberate message pointed out that Muslims and Hindus could go to Saint Louis University, but the Catholic parishioners of the Jesuits in St. Elizabeth's Church, thirteen blocks east of the University, had to go to the University of Illinois to get a degree. Father Holloran's first reaction was one of surprise, but he offered continual support to Father Heithaus. With the urging of the acting Father General, Zaccheus P. Maher, the University integrated that fall.

Under pressure from parents who seemed to think that all their daughters would marry black classmates if they went to an integrated college, Father Holloran decided against allowing the black students to attend the prom. He gave a note to Father Heithaus to put in the school paper. In conscience, Father Heithaus could not do this. Under Jesuit rules, a member could not be ordered to go against his conscience. Father Holloran had to accept Heithaus's refusal. Instead, he ordered him out of the community. The Father Provincial, now Father Joseph P. Zuercher, and his consultors, expelled "Heit" from the Order. They then modified their decision to recognize the position of Father Maher. Father Maher, in turn, suggested a change of residence for Father Heithaus, in order to ensure domestic tranquility, but reprimanded University officials for not facing up to the moral and ethical issues involved.

Saint Louis University had become the first university in a slave state to integrate. Father Heithaus received commendation from prominent Jesuits and the president of the U.S. Chamber of Commerce. But many years would elapse before Father Heithaus would be able to return to the University.

Years later, when he returned to St. Louis, he set out to replace, reorganize, and reassemble material that he had gathered for a museum at the University. The Province at this time was closing its historic Rock building at Florissant, the oldest novitiate in continuous existence in the Order. Father Heithaus proposed a historic museum there. Father Provincial Gerald Sheehan approved his plan, and "Heit" set about building what became the leading religious history museum in the Midwest.

In the years between World Wars I and II, the faculty in the College of Arts and Sciences was excellent. Father William Mc-Gucken was a spokesman for Catholic education with several influential books. Father Raymond Corrigan and Medievalist Herbert Coulson brought prestige to the History Department. Classicists Father Otto Kuhnmuench and Dr. William Korfmacher were able men. Father Kleist wrote Latin textbooks. Father William McCabe headed the English Department before being chosen president of Rockhurst College in Kansas City and then Creighton University in Omaha.

When Father Holloran finished his term as president, Father Paul Reinert, the dean of the College of Arts and Sciences, succeeded him as acting president, and later as president. Reinert was the first person since World War I to rise to the presidency from the lay rather than the seminary sections of the school. Further, Father Reinert was the first president in the long history of the school to boast a degree from a major secular institution, namely, the University of Chicago. He knew American education and was to hold many distinguished positions in and outside the local sphere.

It had been presumed in the Province that Father Reinert would take Father Mc-Gucken's place as province prefect of studies, "Inspector General" of all Jesuit schools in the Midwest. That was not to be. He was to spend his educational efforts at Saint Louis University. He built up an entirely new administrative team.

Father Holloran had close at hand many veterans of the St. Louis educational scene, such as Alumni Director William Ryan, S.J., a widely known former principal of Saint. Louis University High School, and the popular dean of men at Saint Louis University, Father Francis O'Hern. Father Reinert's team had no significant elder statesmen with a knowledge of the local scene.

Reinert overlooked University graduates with local backgrounds, such as Father Louis Barth, Edmund Burke, who had won the Silver Star for bravery in the Pacific War, and Richard Cahill, former president of Saint Louis University High School, who became a distinguished pastor in Milwaukee.

Reinert took his principal assistant from graduate studies and his representative at the Medical School from the same recently ordained class, fine young men and astute philosophers, but without degrees and established reputations. Further, neither was capable of wide friendships and seemed to be unconcerned that they were not easily approachable or widely known.

The dean of the Graduate School was even more of a problem. He finished his degree in Toronto and was appointed superior of the scholastics at the University. He had to be removed after only six months in office for bullying the students. In spite of the Father Provincial's firing of "Bully Bob," Reinert insisted on naming him dean of the Graduate School against the unanimous vote of his twelve Jesuit brethren on the Board of Consultors.

"Bully Bob"—as the scholastics called him—was convinced that Science did not belong on a Jesuit campus. He closed the Dental School and the Institute of Technology, founded by Father James Macelwane, the leading seismologist in the country. He tried to close Parks College but was baffled by the evasive response of Father John Choppesky, a slow-acting but astute Arkansan.

Two efforts to sell Parks failed: once, when the faculty at the University of Illinois–Edwardsville pointed out that 80 percent of the Parks students were not natives of Illinois; later, when the state government turned down an offer. Behind the scenes, apparently, was the powerful influence of Congressman Mel Price of the East Side, a graduate of the University, who wished to keep in his area this great school.

Holloran had seen the basketball program grow into national prominence under Coach John Flanagan and superstar "Easy" Ed Macauley. Holloran hoped to have a successful football team by hiring a professional-type coach. The man talked a good game but couldn't fill the stadium. Reinert allowed the basketball team, now highly successful, to continue, and saw the development of a sound championship soccer program, working with local coaches Bob Goelker and Harry Keough and local stars led by Pat McBride and Al Trost. Pat

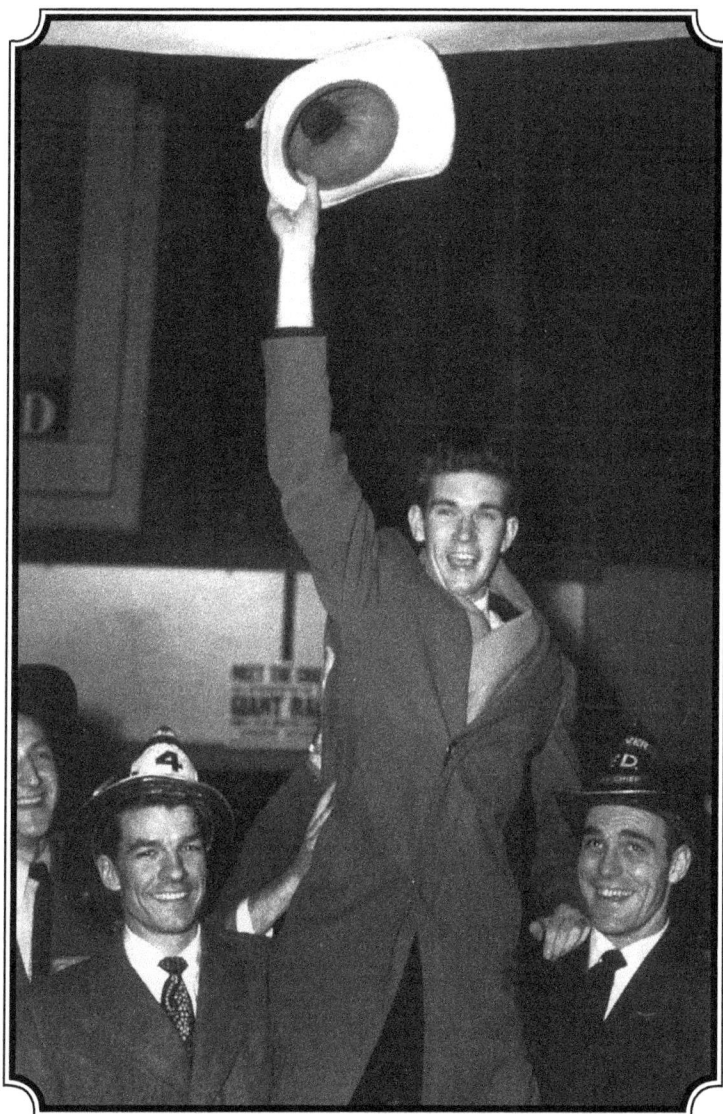

Ed Macauley and the triumphant Billikens in 1948.

WILLIAM BARNABY FAHERTY, S.J.

1978 St. Louis University "

BACK ROW — left to right: Val Pelizzaro (Assistant Coach), Joe Filla
Dave Kuenzle, Mark Schell, Chris Miller, Jeff Lagrand, Jim Tietjens
Dan Doran, Frank Schuler, Harry Keough (Head Coach), Miguel de Lima
Assistant Coach).

WILLIAM BARNABY FAHERTY, S.J.

40

kens"

NT ROW — left to right: Ty Keough, Larry Hulcer, Don Huber,
Malle, Tom Tangaro, John Hayes, Dennis Seerey, Mark Frederickson,
Pelizzaro.

WILLIAM BARNABY FAHERTY, S.J.

41

Leahy starred in professional football, but Reinert ended the failing football program on campus.

The Arts College faculty in the years immediately after World War II matched that of the 1930s. Father Walter Ong gained wide acclaim for his analyses of the changes in understanding that came with the move from oral to written communication brought on by advances in printing.

Father John Francis Bannon became the leader of an entire group of historians who had studied under Herbert Bolton at the University of California. They specialized in the frontiers where Spanish and English colonies met—Florida and the Southwest—and won the name "Spanish Borderlands" scholars.

Further, Father Bannon was the only Jesuit whose textbooks were used in secular schools. Thomas P. Neill published textbooks in use chiefly in Catholic Colleges. Clement Mihanovich and William Monahan taught sociology. James Collins and Vernon Bourke gained recognition in the area of philosophy.

Father Paul Reinert had been University president and superior of the Jesuit Community since 1939. It became clear that a six-year term for a college president was not enough. But it was enough for the position of community superior. Other schools, such as Notre Dame, realized the need of a longer term for the president but did not retain him as community superior. Saint Louis University did. It kept Father Reinert in both positions throughout the 1950s and then the anniversary years of the 1960s.

St. Louis City celebrated its two hundredth anniversary in 1964, and the University its 150th year in 1968.

I had come to Saint Louis University in 1963 from Queen's Work Publishing House to write the history of the school. I taught only one class each semester. I finished the book for the University's 150th anniversary celebration in 1968 under the title *Better the Dream: Saint Louis University and Community, 1818–1968*. I took my title from Professor John Knoepfle's poem, written for the occasion, "Lines for Men of the Greater Interior." A pictorial accompanied my book. Mine held no illustrations. Lewis Mayhew called it "excellent history" in his annual appraisal of books on education.

In the anniversary year also, Father Reinert added laymen to the Board of Trustees.

Over the years, Dr. Carroll Hochwalt, vice president of Monsanto, had headed the President's Council. When the time came for ex-

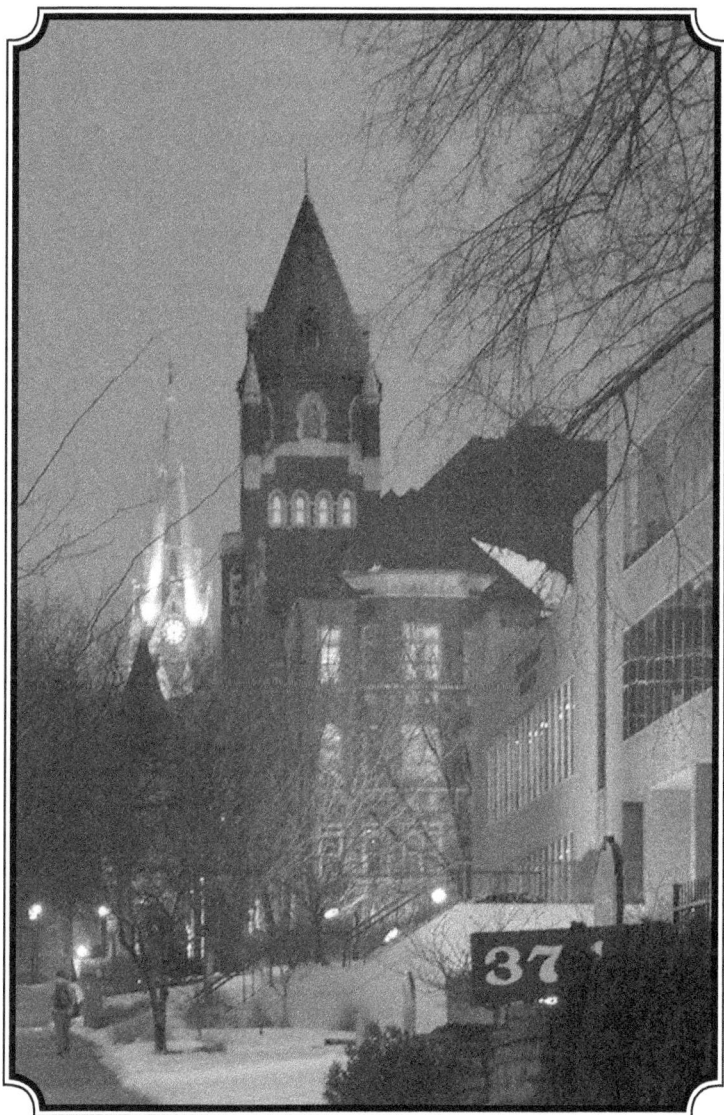

Lindell Boulevard

WILLIAM BARNABY FAHERTY, S.J.

45

panding the Board of Trustees to include lay-men, it was widely presumed that Hochwalt would head the Board. Instead, Reinert took a man with no industrial connections, Daniel Schlafly, head of the School Board of St. Louis City and a graduate of Georgetown.

Through the long winter of 1973–74, the University search committee sought a successor to Reinert. They interviewed college presidents from the eastern seaboard but generally ignored local applicants. Most of the people who might have wanted the position would not accept the arrangement that Reinert was still powerful. Rumor had it that one of the best, the president of Loyola in Baltimore, would take the job only if Father Reinert went on a leave of absence for a year or took an office away from the University for the inner-city work he wanted to do.

Father Faherty; Mary Arnoldy, a student; and Dr. Irvin Arkin discuss "Theology of Woman," mid-1960s.

Finally, under pressure from the Jesuit Provincial, Father Leo Weber, Father Dan O'Connell, a low-key psychology professor who had not even applied, was chosen. He had limited administrative experience beyond the year as superior of the Jesuit community at the University. A popular teacher and counselor, he had won the Nancy Mc-Neir Ring Award for outstanding teaching in 1967. Readily accessible, he had lived in a student dormitory for two years before being named superior of the community at Jesuit Hall. Now as president, he would remain accessible. He decided to move back into an undergraduate residence hall. He planned to drive a Volkswagen as the official presidential car.

A graduate of Saint Louis University High School and of Saint Louis University, O'Connell had taken his doctorate in general experimental psychology at the

Father Paul Reinert, S.J., at far right.

WILLIAM BARNABY FAHERTY, S.J.

University of Illinois in 1963 and spent two years at the Harvard University Center for Cognitive Studies as a National Science Foundation doctoral fellow. He then won international recognition in the field of Psycholinguistics, the study of the relationship between language and the behavioral characteristics of those doing it. His considerable credentials gave him a high rung on the academic ladder.

A full photograph on the front page of the summer edition of the *Saint Louis University Magazine* presented a handsome man of average weight and height, with a friendly smile, dark-rimmed glasses, and a slight tuft of dark hair on the forehead, a remnant of a once vigorous thatch. His entire manner evoked confidence. One could easily meet and instantly trust the man.

The editors of the *Magazine* had previ-

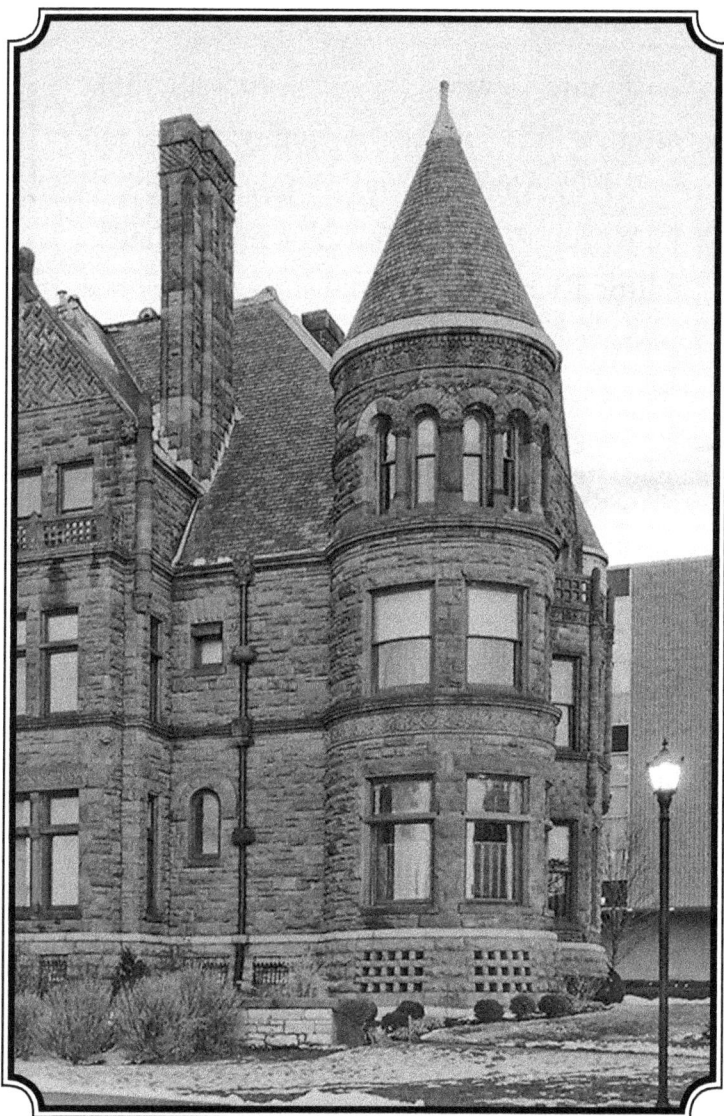

Cupples House

WILLIAM BARNABY FAHERTY, S.J.

ously interviewed O'Connell back in 1966, after he had joined the faculty, and again in 1972. Alumnae and alumni wanted to know more about him. Not unexpectedly, editor Rich Roberts published a two-hour interview with O'Connell in the July 1974 issue. Independent Dean Leon Stelzer of Parks showed himself immediately to be one of the few University administrators always respectful of the new president. The others presumed Father Reinert was still the boss. Only John Cardinal Carberry, the archbishop of St. Louis, among important office-holding individuals, seemed to match Stelzer in his public recognition of President O'Connell.

In the last year of Reinert's administration, his choice of vice president for Academic Affairs, a fellow Jesuit, had ended the Baccalaureate and the Mass of the Holy Spirit. Further, he removed all religious symbols from the University classrooms. O'Connell immediately reversed that whole pattern.

While Reinert was unconcerned about Parks, O'Connell was rightly interested. He had often come to the school to take his nephew Edward Sabin's psychology class.

There was one important thing Father Reinert had not mentioned to Dan O'Connell. It was this: The University had become bankrupt. O'Connell found this out, as did the other members of the faculty, in the writings of a member of the Board on the development of universities of the time. She said it not in criticism, but as singling out the frankness of Father Reinert in dealing with his constituents.

After two years, several members of the Board of Trustees approached Father O'Connell and said they were bringing in a successor in the fall. O'Connell resigned immediately. Father Edmund Drummond, the provincial's assistant for Academic Affairs, agreed to take the position for one year.

An experienced administrator, Father Thomas Fitzgerald of Fairfield University, then accepted the post. In a few years he put the school "in the black" and arranged for economic stability. He welcomed the Aquinas Institute of Theology that moved from Dubuque. Then he returned to his Province to teach the Classics.

Lawrence Biondi was known at Saint Louis University before he became president. He had been a member of the Board and created friendly relations with a number of people in the community. He was a native of Chicago, with a doctorate from Georgetown.

His term was a term of action. There

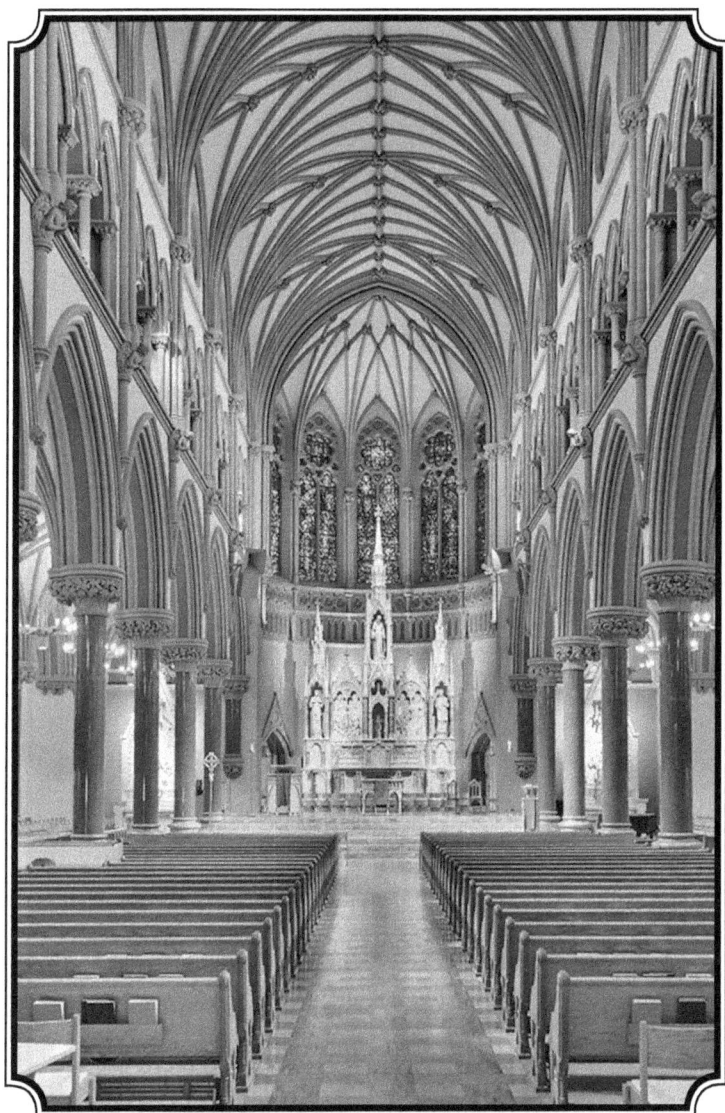

St. Francis Xavier interior

WILLIAM BARNABY FAHERTY, S.J.

was some program underway at all times. First, he closed Parks College in Cahokia and established the Aeronautical Engineering School in a building on Lindell east of Tegger Hall, a gift of local aviation leaders. He looked to clarifying the boundaries of the school that hitherto had been uncertain, by arches over Grand Avenue at Market, Lafayette, and various places on Grand Avenue, and by fences, gateways, and arches on the campus itself. In general, he beautified the campus with hundreds of new trees, fountains, ponds, statues, and fences.

He turned the impressive St. Louis Club on the north side of Lindell, across from the Commerce School, into a museum of art. It had served as offices of the Graduate School. The new museum features a display of Jesuit memorabilia that Father Heithaus had gathered over the years and housed in the Jesuit Museum of History at Florissant.

With a surprise gift from a slightly known alumnus of the University, Dr. Richard Chaifetz, Father Biondi was able to bless a magnificent dome-shaped arena for basketball and other sports. He opened many student residences on Pine Street between Spring and Vandeventer.

During his time, the tar and asphalt campus had become a garden in the center of the city. Through the generosity of the Cook family, a spacious assembly hall and impressive entranceway graced the west side of the Davis-Shaughnessy Building. He also built two three-story carports, one on the south side of Laclede just west of Grand, the other at Compton and Olive on the northeast corner of the campus.

In short, the campus was enlarged, enriched, and made clearly visible in the Midtown area west of the city. Buildings that had been on Lindell in front of St. Francis Xavier Church had gone down, and in place a park with a beautiful fountain. As one drove west on Olive, he enjoyed a view of the extremely beautiful French Gothic College Church of St. Francis Xavier.

About
the Author

Over the past forty years, Father William Barnaby Faherty, S.J., has received invitations to write the story of the most important botanical garden in the world and its founder, Henry Shaw; of the most influential flight school and its chief, Oliver Lafayette Parks; of space exploration at NASA's installation in Florida; of the St. Louis archdiocese; and of the city of St. Louis itself. *St. Louis: A Concise History*, co-authored with neighborhood specialist NiNi Harris, is in its fourth edition.

Following the advice of one of his mentors, Pulitzer Prize–winner Paul Horgan, Faherty tried his hand several times with fiction. MGM adapted his first novel, *A Wall for San*

WILLIAM BARNABY FAHERTY, S.J.

Sebastian, for a movie. His third novel, *The Call of Pope Octavian*, tells of a future pope who updates the administrative machinery of the Papacy as Vatican II has updated external attitudes. The Missouri Writers' Guild has rated several of his books the best work of the year. His *St. Louis Irish: An Unmatched Celtic Community* and *The St. Louis German Catholics* documented the history of two strong St. Louis ethnic communities. Most recently, Father Faherty released *Catholic St. Louis: A Pictorial History*, with Mark Scott Abeln.

A native of St. Louis of Irish-Alsatian ancenstry, Father Faherty received a Doctor of Philosophy degree in History at Saint Louis University in 1949. Rockhurst University conferred on him an honorary Doctorate in Humane Letters in 1993, and the Aquinas Institute honored him with a degree in 2007.

www.ingramcontent.com/pod-product-compliance
Lightning Source LLC
Chambersburg PA
CBHW071423040426
42445CB00012BA/1280